Introduction

'The principal focus of mathematics teaching in key stage 1 is to ensure that pupils develop confidence and mental fluency with whole numbers.'

Key Stage 1 National Curriculum Programme of Study

'The teacher created a positive climate for learning in which pupils were interested and engaged.'

OFSTED Inspector

Welcome to a world of mathematical fun and games!

Easy to play and requiring only basic equipment, these educational games engage even the most reluctant of learners whilst boosting confidence for all.

Great for teachers, intervention workers, teaching assistants, private tutors and parents, the flexible nature of this game pack offers:

- practice for specific objectives from the new National Curriculum
- a great resource to:
  "ensure students are engaged in learning and generate high levels of commitment to learning"
  (Outstanding Grade Descriptors, *Ofsted School Inspection Handbook* (updated 2014))
- the opportunity to demonstrate a commitment to:
  "the social development of pupils at the school" within curriculum time
  (Ofsted Framework for School Inspection (updated 2014))
- an effective assessment tool
- the promotion of problem solving and thinking skills through game strategy
- fun homework activities

Playing Information

All these games require a pack of playing cards and most also need some kind of coloured counters or other objects such as beads or buttons. Suitable materials are available from Tarquin - see page 40 for details. When the picture cards are used the jack represents number eleven, the queen is number twelve and the king is thirteen. To help children remember this you may want to consider writing the actual numbers in the corners of each card.

And that's all you need to know to enjoy years of happy gaming!

David Smith

Take 2

Focus

Take Two is a game for two or more players which practices saying one more and one less than a number up to ten.

What you need

- Playing cards (aces to tens of two suits)

How to play

Remove two complete suits of cards and then also the picture cards of the remaining two suits. Lay the rest of the cards in front of the players as shown.

Player 1 turns over a single card and says the number shown. They must then say what is one more and one less than that number.

For example

Player 1 turns over a four they must say three (one less) and five (one more).

Player 1 then turns over another card to see if they can find a three or a five to make a pair of numbers that have a difference of one. If successful in finding a matching pair Player 1 keeps the two cards in front of them. If the numbers are not one more or less than each other, the cards are turned back over and put back in the same places.

Player 2 then turns over a nine. Player 2 has to say eight and ten before turning over their second card to try and find a number one less or more than nine.

Players continue to turn over cards to try and find pairs that are one more or less than each other. Keep playing until all the cards have been used or until no more pairs can be made.

How to win

The player with the most pairs in front of them is the winner.

Rule changes / Next steps

- Players turn a card and say how many more to make ten. They then have to try and turn a card over with that value to make a pair.

ACE Mathematics Games 1

16 exciting activities to engage ages 5–6

David Smith

tarquin

Acknowledgements

Thanks are due to many people but especially to my lovely wife and also my dear mum who between them patiently played all the games with me to test their initial suitability. I also have to thank the teachers and children of Peel Park Primary School for giving them a road test, spotting my errors and making suggestions on how they could be further developed and improved. Finally thanks go to the staff at Tarquin, for their support in the editing process.

Dedication

This book is dedicated to the memory of Maxine Firth, an inspirational friend and colleague who shared my ideal of an enjoyment of mathematics for all.

Published by Tarquin Publications
Suite 74, 17 Holywell Hill
St Albans
AL1 1DT

www.tarquingroup.com

Distributed in the USA by Parkwest
www.parkwestpubs.com
www.amazon.com & major retailers

Distributed in Australia by OLM www.lat-olm.com.au

ISBN: 978-1-907-55091-1

Printed and designed in the United Kingdom

Target

Focus

Target is a game for two or more players which practices saying one more or one less than numbers up to ten.

What you need

- Playing cards (picture cards removed)
- Target game board

▶ How to play

Before play can begin, three cards must be turned over and placed face-up in each space on the game board. The rest of the cards are dealt out equally between the players and are then placed face-down in a pile in front of them, as shown in the diagram below.

Player 2

TARGET

Player 1

Player 3

Player 1 then turns over a card from their pile and looks to see if they have a number which is one more or one less than a number on the game board.

For example

Player 1 first turns over a seven and places it on top of the eight of spades, as seven is one less than eight. Then Player 1 turns over an ace and places it on top of the two of clubs as the ace (one) is one less than two. Player 1 then turns over a three and can't place this card on the game board. When this happens the card is placed face-up next to their pile and this is the end of their turn.

Player 2

TARGET

Player 1

Player 3

Player 2 then turns over a card and tries to find a number which is one more or less than a number on the game board. In this example Player 2 turns over the eight of clubs. This card can be placed on top of the seven of hearts as eight is one more than seven. Player 2 then turns over the two of clubs and places it on top of the ace. Next a five is turned over but this can't be placed anywhere on the game board.

Player 3 then takes their turn. The first card turned over is the six of diamonds which can't be placed on the target game board. However, the card can be placed on top of Player 2's five of spades as six is one more than five. Player 3 can then turn over another card to see if it can be placed on the game board or on top of another player's pile. This time it is an eight so Player 3's turn comes to an end.

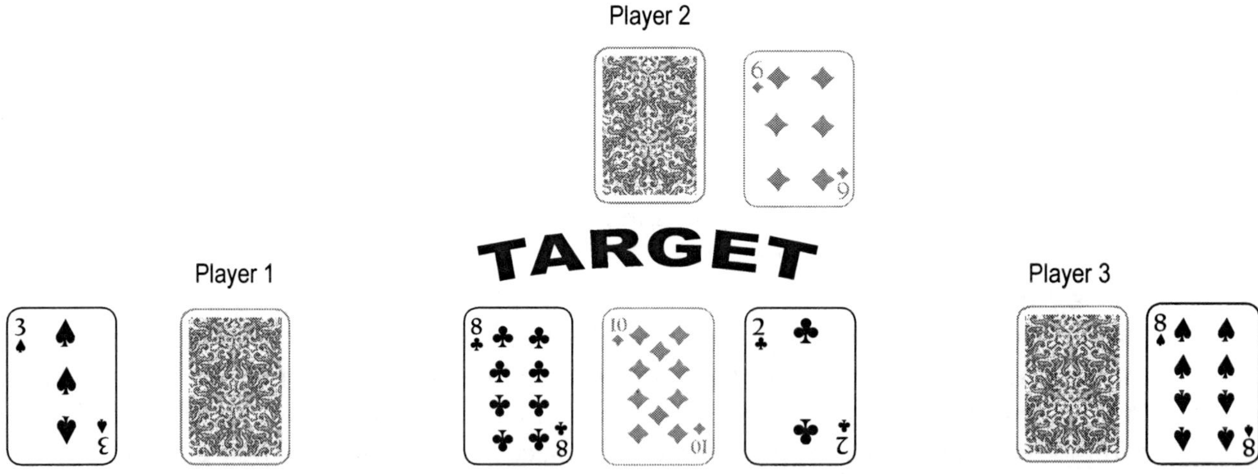

When players have their next turns they can look at their face up card first to see if that will go on any of the cards on the game board before turning a card over. Player 1 can therefore put their three on top of the two as three is one more than two.

How to win

The first player to use all the cards in their pile is the winner. If the players get to a point where they all still have cards in their pile but none of them can take a turn, the player with the fewest number of cards is the winner.

Rule changes / Next steps

- Include the picture cards and play one more or one less up to thirteen.
- Play two more or two less.

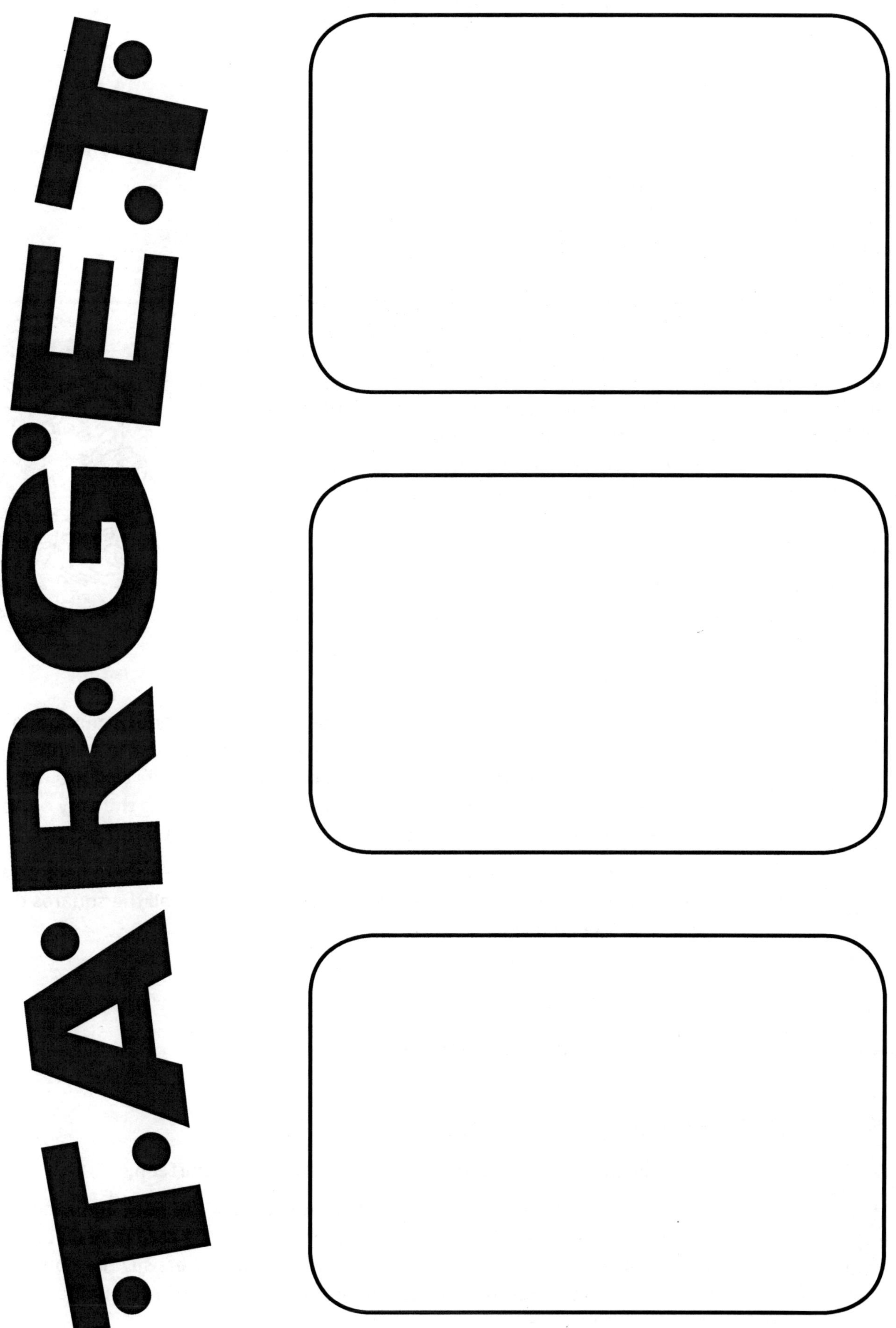
T.A.R.G.E.T.

Robot Wars

Focus

Robot Wars is a game for two or more players which practices recognising and saying one more or one less than numbers up to twenty.

What you need

- Playing cards (picture cards removed)
- Counters (a different colour for each player)
- Robot Wars game board

How to play

When the picture cards have been removed, the remaining cards are shuffled and placed face-down, within reach of all the players. Player 1 turns over a card and says the number. They can then say either one more or one less than the number on the card, and Player 1 writes this number into one of the empty spaces on the Robot Wars game board. So if the number seven is turned over, they can write down either the number six (one less) or the number eight (one more) in any of the blank squares on the robot.

Player 2 then turns over a card and says one more or one less than that number. They can write the number in any of the remaining blank squares on the board.

Players continue to take turns, saying one more or less and writing their number on the board.

		6	
			10
7	7		

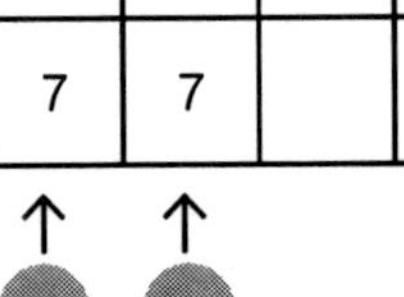

However, if a player can write their number next to an identical number already on the board (such as a seven next to a seven or a three next to a three) they can then cover both those numbers with counters. Numbers that are not identical cannot be written in an adjacent square unless it is the only option left on the board. If a player is able to place counters they get another turn.

When all the cards have been used, mix them up and place them back down in a pile within reach of all the players. Play continues until all the squares on the board have been used.

How to win

The player with the most counters on the robot is the winner.

Rule changes / Next steps

- Include the picture cards and play with numbers up to thirteen.
- The tens as well as the picture cards are removed from the pack and each player starts with an ace in front of them. When a player turns over a card they place it next to the ace to make a number from eleven up to nineteen. Players say the number they have made and then the number that is one more or one less. Write numbers and place counters in the same way as previously described.

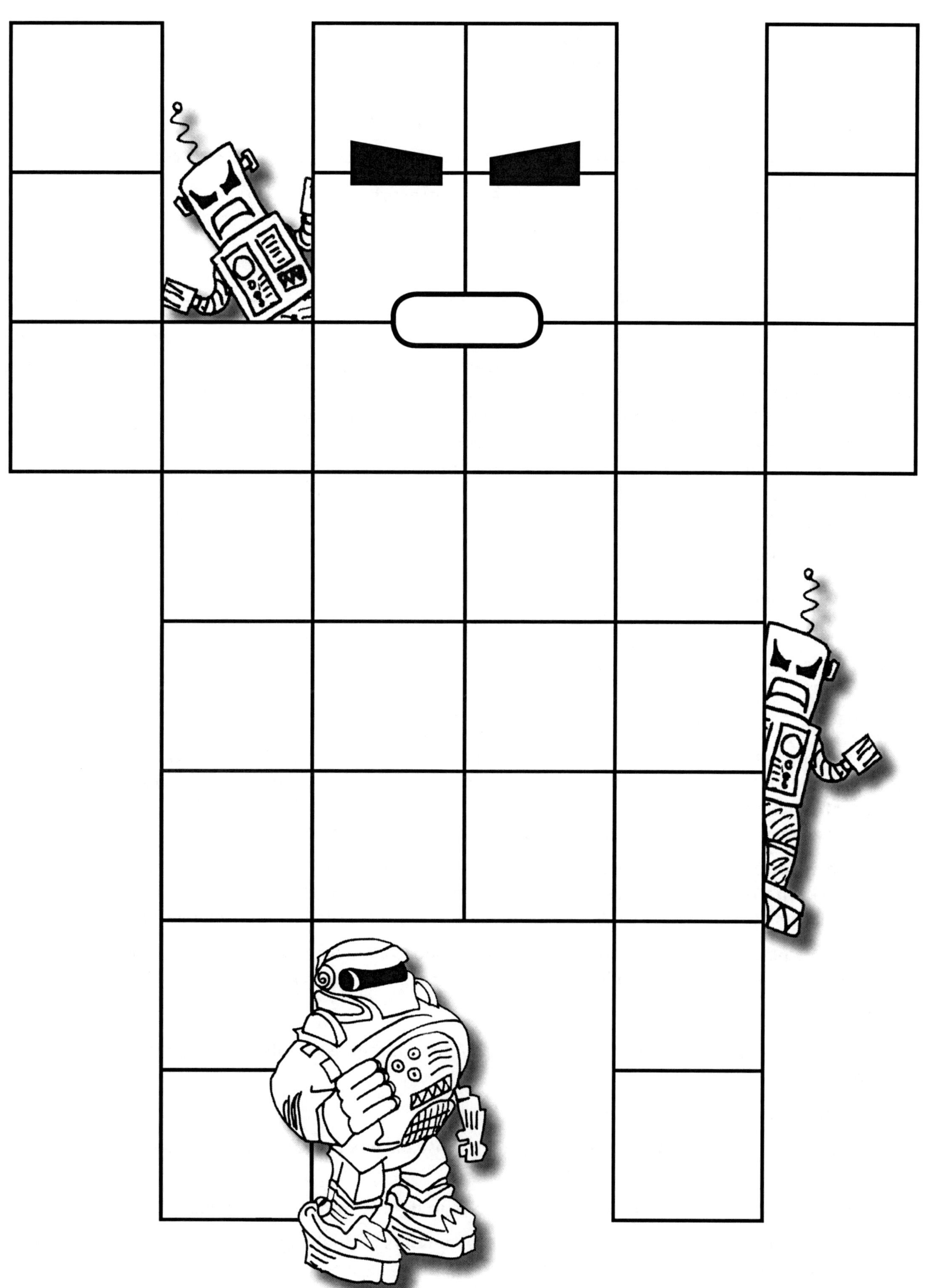

Double Trouble

Focus

Double Trouble is a game for two or more players which practices doubling numbers up to ten.

What you need

- Playing cards (picture cards removed)
- Counters

How to play

When the tens and picture cards have been removed from the pack the remaining cards are shuffled. Player 1 deals two cards to themselves and one card to every other player. The other players look at their card and double the number shown, keeping the answer to themselves. Player 1 can then turn over one of their cards and say the double. They can then choose to stick with this card or put it down and pick up the other card to double. The players then put down their cards in turn and say their doubles. The player with the highest total wins all the cards from the other players and places them in a pile in front of them.

For example

Player 1

Player 2

Player 3

Player 1 above turned over their first card (a three) and because this is a low card decided to turn over their second card, an eight. The players then put down their cards and say the doubles of 'double 8 is 16' (Player 1), 'double 9 is 18' (Player 2) and 'double 6 is 12' (Player 3). So Player 2 wins this round and collects all the cards to put in a pile in front of them.

Player 2 then deals, with two in front of them and one for each of the other players. Player 2 decides whether to keep their first card or change it. If their second card is smaller they can't change back to the first one. Players put down their cards and say the double with the highest total winning the round.

If two or more players have the same total then that round is a draw and the cards are placed together to carry on into the next round and be won by the player who has the highest double.

How to win

The player who has won the most cards after a set number of rounds, or when the pack is finished, wins the game.

Rule changes / Next steps

- If two or more players have the same total then those players take another card from the pack and the player with the highest double total wins.
- Leave the picture cards in so that the players have to double some larger numbers.
- Discuss using their knowledge of doubling these numbers to doubling two digit multiples of ten. For example, double four is eight so double forty is eighty.

Cover Up

Focus

Cover Up is a game for up to four players which practices adding and subtracting numbers up to ten.

What you need

- Playing cards (picture cards removed)
- Counters
- Cover Up game board
- Whiteboard / paper and pen

How to play

When the picture cards have been removed from the pack, three cards are dealt to each player and the remaining cards are placed in a pile, face-down and within reach of all the players. Players must then look at their cards and try to find ways of making one of the numbers on their row. Player 1 goes first and must place any two cards face-up in front of them to match a number on their row.

For example

Player 1 puts down different combinations of these cards to make any of the following possible numbers:

6 + 3 = 9   6 − 3 = 3   8 − 6 = 2   8 − 3 = 5

The other players must check that the calculation is correct, and if so Player 1 can place a counter onto the number on their row. Player 1 then picks up two more cards from the top of the pack to replace the cards they used, and starts to look to see if they can make a different answer ready for their next turn.

Play continues with players taking it in turns to put cards down to try and make different answers. Only one number can be covered with a counter on each turn. If a player can't make a number on their row they can choose to change one, two or all three of their cards instead. They place the cards they don't want on the bottom of the central pile and take the same number of new cards from the top. However, this exchange of cards counts as the player's turn: they are not allowed to try to place a counter. When the cards in the middle run out the next player picks up all those in front of each player, shuffles them and places them back face-down in a pile again.

How to win

The first player to cover all the numbers on their row with a counter is the winner.

Rule changes / Next steps

- If a player puts down two cards of the same value (two twos or two fours) when making an answer they can perform a 'double' trick. This means that as well as placing a counter on their own Cover Up number row they can also remove any one counter from another player's row.
- Allow players to put down three cards at a time to make a number on their row, such as a four, a two and an ace to calculate 4 + 2 − 1 = 5, 4 − 2 − 1 = 1 or 4 + 1 + 2 = 7. The player must then pick up another three cards from the top of the pile.

1	2	3	4	5	6	7	8	9	10

COVER UP

COVER UP

COVER UP

COVER UP

1	2	3	4	5	6	7	8	9	10

1	2	3	4	5	6	7	8	9	10

1	2	3	4	5	6	7	8	9	10

Tower Power

Focus

Tower Power is a game for two or more players which practises adding and subtracting numbers up to ten.

What you need

- Playing cards
- Counters

How to play

The cards are shuffled and five cards are dealt to each player. The rest of the pack is placed face-down and within reach of all the players.

Player 1 turns over a card from the top of the pack and places it face-up in clear view of everyone. All the players must then look at their cards and try to find ways of making the same number. Players can use any two cards and add or subtract them to make the number on the card.

For example

Player 1 turns over a six. Players have to combine their cards to try and make that total, such as:

8 – 2 = 6

10 – 4 = 6

5 + 1 = 6

Players must place their combinations face-up in front of them for everyone to see and check that they are correct. Each player is allowed to place down more than one combination, as long as they make six, but can only use each card once. They can then take a counter for each correct calculation they make and use them to start building a tower. Players then pick up all their cards so they still have the same five cards in their hand for the next turn.

If a player can't find any ways of making the target number they can choose to change any one or two cards from their hand with one or two from the top of the pile.

Play continues until a card the same as a previous number is turned over. All the cards are then collected from the players and shuffled, and five cards each are dealt again for the game to continue as before.

How to win

The first player to power up their tower to ten counters is the winner.

Rule changes / Next steps

- If there are only two players the cards used for calculations can be left on the table after each turn. Each player is then given the same number of cards from the top of the pack as they have used, ready for the next turn.
- Allow players to use three cards to make a number, such as an ace, a two and a three to make six as 1 + 2 + 3 = 6.

Flamingo Bingo

Focus

Flamingo Bingo is a game for two or more players which practices adding and subtracting numbers up to ten.

What you need

- Playing cards
- Counters
- Flamingo Bingo cards
- Whiteboard / paper and pen

How to play

Each player needs to start the game with a Flamingo Bingo card, five counters and a whiteboard or paper and pen. The cards are shuffled and placed in a pile, face-down and within reach of all the players. Player 1 starts the game by turning over three cards. All players then use these three numbers in different ways, using only addition and subtraction, to try and make a number on their game card.

For example

Player 1 turns over a four, a two and a seven. Different numbers can be made as follows:

4 + 2 = 6 7 − 2 = 5 7 − 4 = 3 4 − 2 = 2

Players need to write down their calculation on paper or a whiteboard to show how they made the number on their bingo card and then cover it with a counter. A time limit of ten, twenty or thirty seconds needs to be placed on players to make a number. A player can only place one counter for each round. If a player can't think of a way to make an uncovered number, they can't place a counter for that round.

Play continues with players taking turns to put three cards face-up for all players to try and make another number on their card.

How to win

Players have to achieve a 'full house' by covering every number on their card. The first player to stand on one leg and shout 'Flamingo Bingo' (not compulsory!) is the winner. Player's calculations are checked at the end of the game to make sure they are correct.

Rule changes / Next steps

- Have one player as a referee who turns over cards and checks answers. Play as a whole class by having one bingo card between two or use the spare cards to make one each.
- Use objects such as counters, cubes, buttons or even dried beans to help players with their adding and subtracting.

0
4
5
7
10

2
5
7
9
10

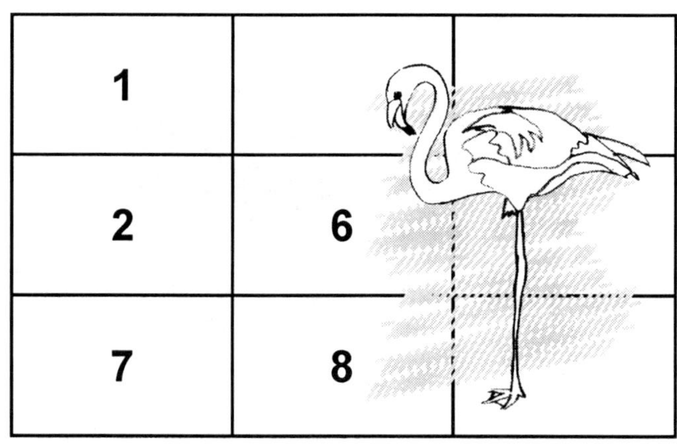
1
2
6
7
8

2
3
6
7
10

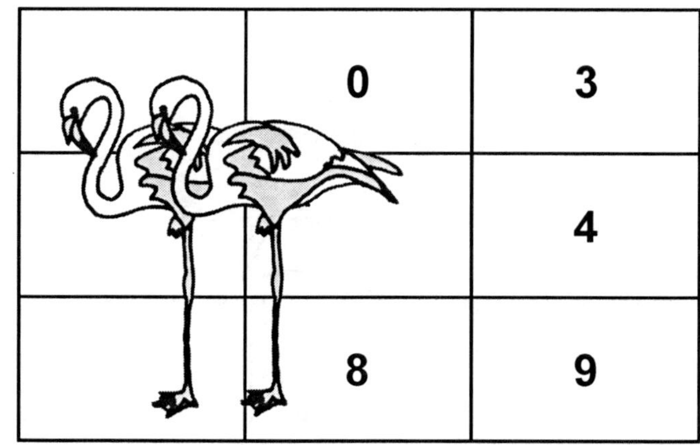
0
3
4
8
9

1
3
4
6
9

0
1
5
6
10

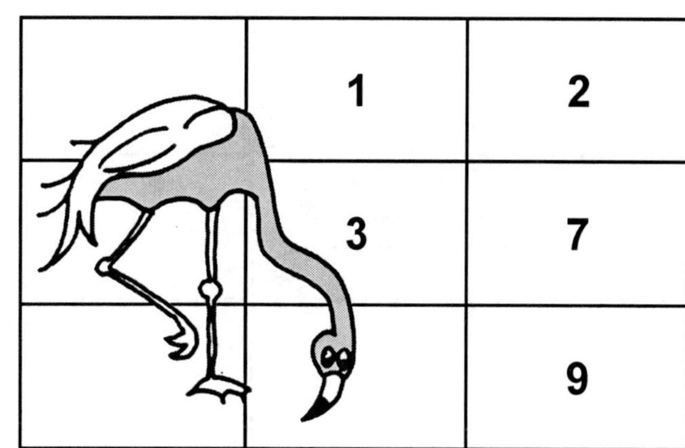
1
2
3
7
9

2
4
5
8
9

0
2
3
6
9

0
3
6
7
10

1
2
5
8
10

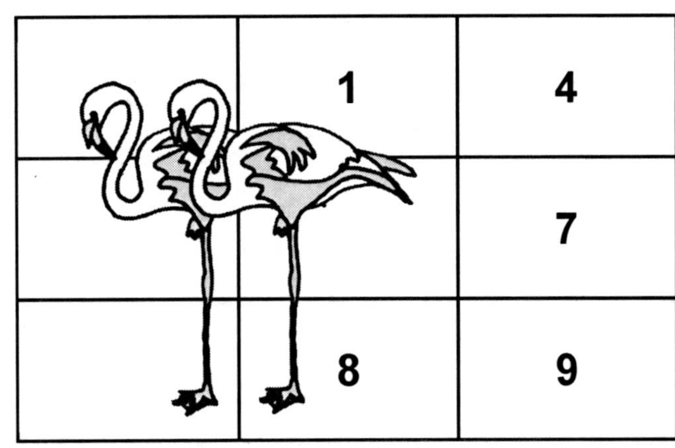
1
4
7
8
9

0
3
5
8
10

0
2
4
6
9

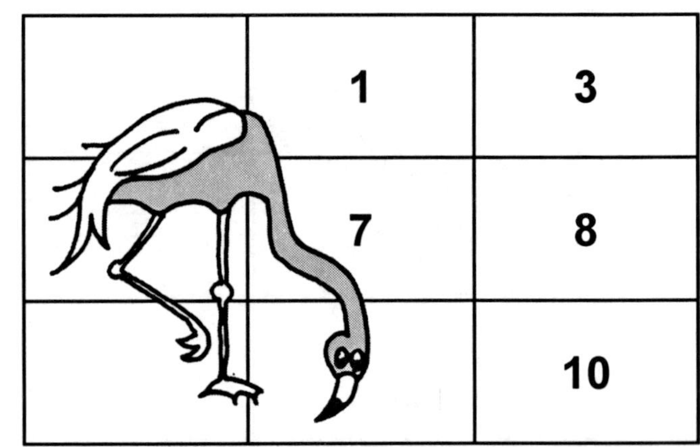
1
3
7
8
10

Worms

Focus

Worms is a game for two or more players which practices recall of addition and subtraction facts up to fifteen.

What you need

- ▶ Playing cards (picture cards removed)
- ▶ Counters (different colour for each player)
- ▶ Worms game board

How to play

When the picture cards have been removed the remaining cards are placed face-down in a pile within reach of all the players. Player 1 turns over a card and says the number. They then have to say how many more they would add to that number to make ten.

For example

Player 1 turns over a six, and has to say 6 + 4 = 10. They can then place a counter on any matching answer of four on the game board.

Then Player 2 turns over an ace and has to say 1 + 9 = 10 before placing a counter on any matching answer of nine on the game board.

Players continue to take turns saying how many more to make ten and cover matching answers on the game board with their counters. Each player must try and make a worm by placing counters on adjacent squares, as shown in the diagram. If a player can't make an answer on the game board they miss that turn.

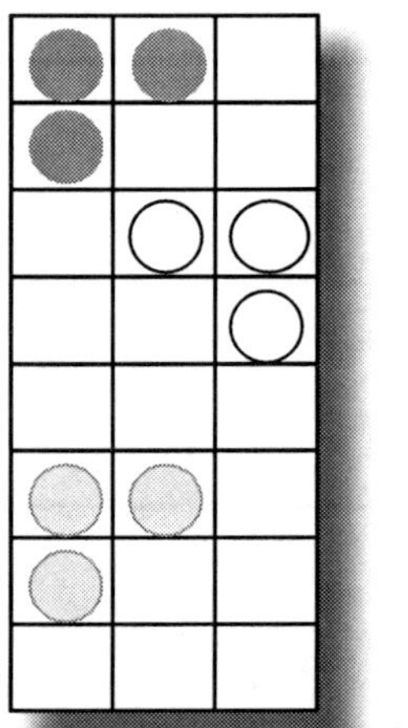

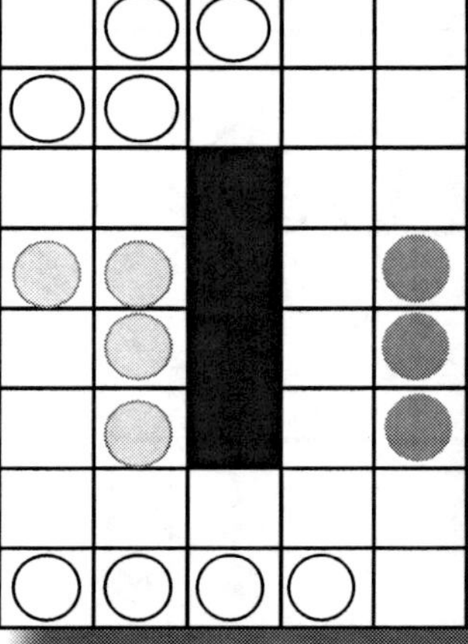

How to win

For two players, the first to get four counters together on adjacent squares wins the game. For more than two players, the first to get three counters together on adjacent squares wins the game.

Rule changes / Next steps

- ▶ Do calculations as subtraction from ten, such as 10 – 6 = 4 or 10 – 1 = 9.
- ▶ Play Worms 15 by allowing players to turn over two cards and either add the value of the cards together to find the total or subtract the smaller value from the larger to find the difference. For example, if Player 1 turns over a six and a nine then that player would have to say 6 + 9 = 15 or 9 – 6 = 3. They can then place a counter on either of the matching answers on the game board.
- ▶ You could also allow play to continue until all the squares on the board have been covered, or a set number of counters used, especially if there are only two players. Then add up the final score for each player to decide the winner using the following points:

3 square worm = 2 points
4 square worm = 5 points
5 square worm = 10 points
6 square worm = 20 points

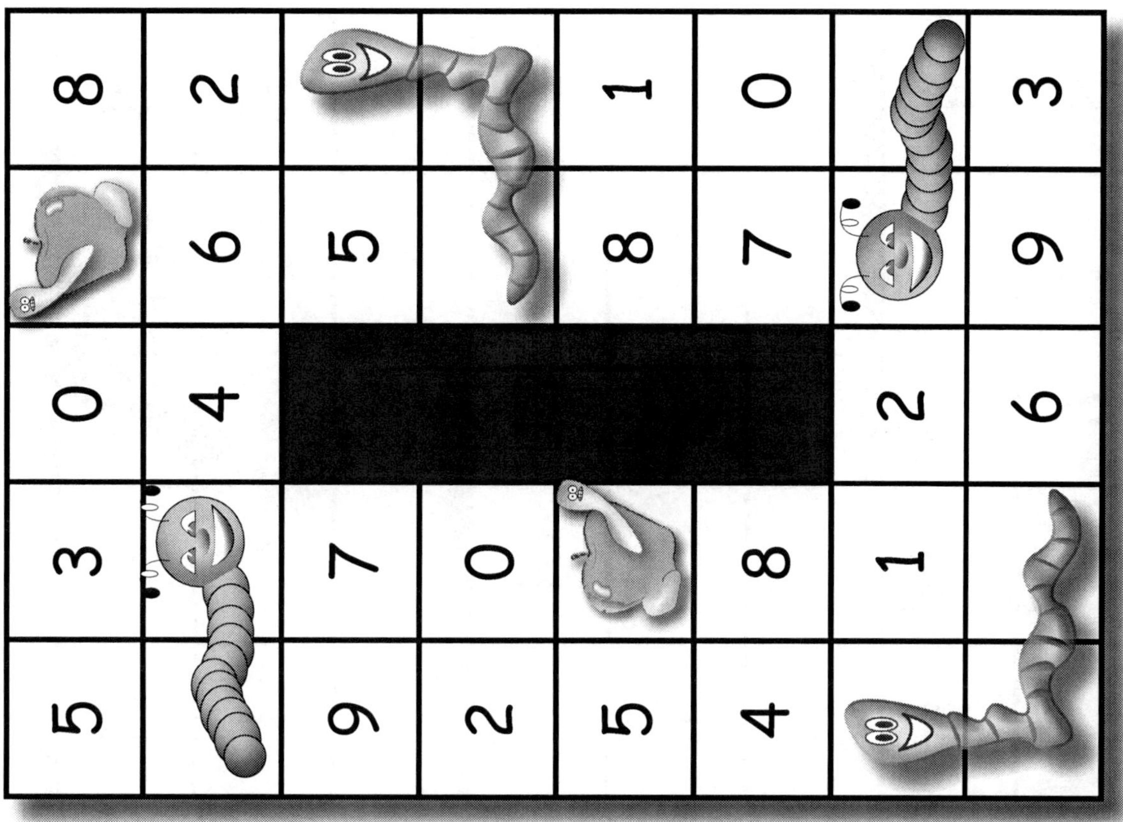

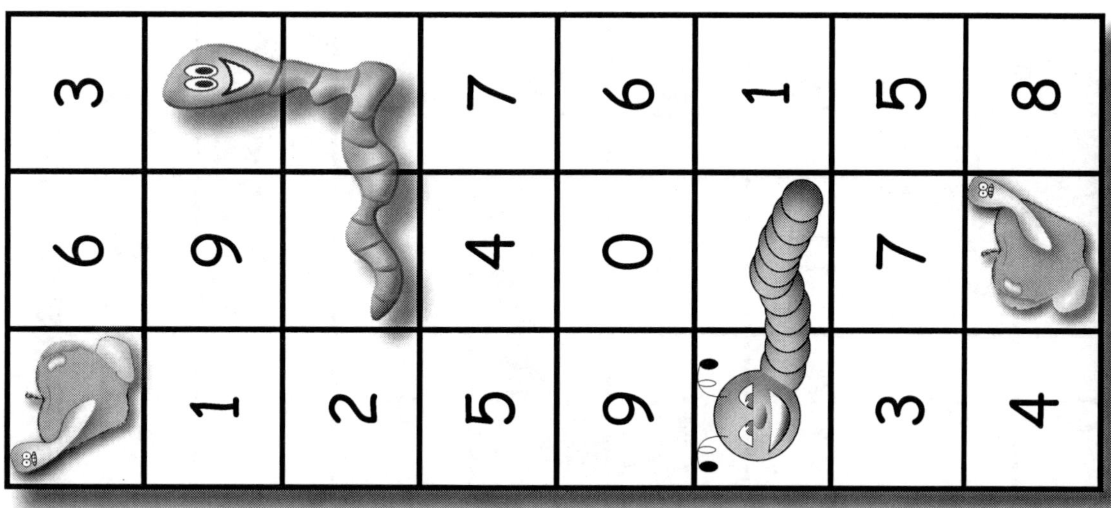

0		
8		
13	11	5
	2	10
		14
9	3	6
7		
12	4	1

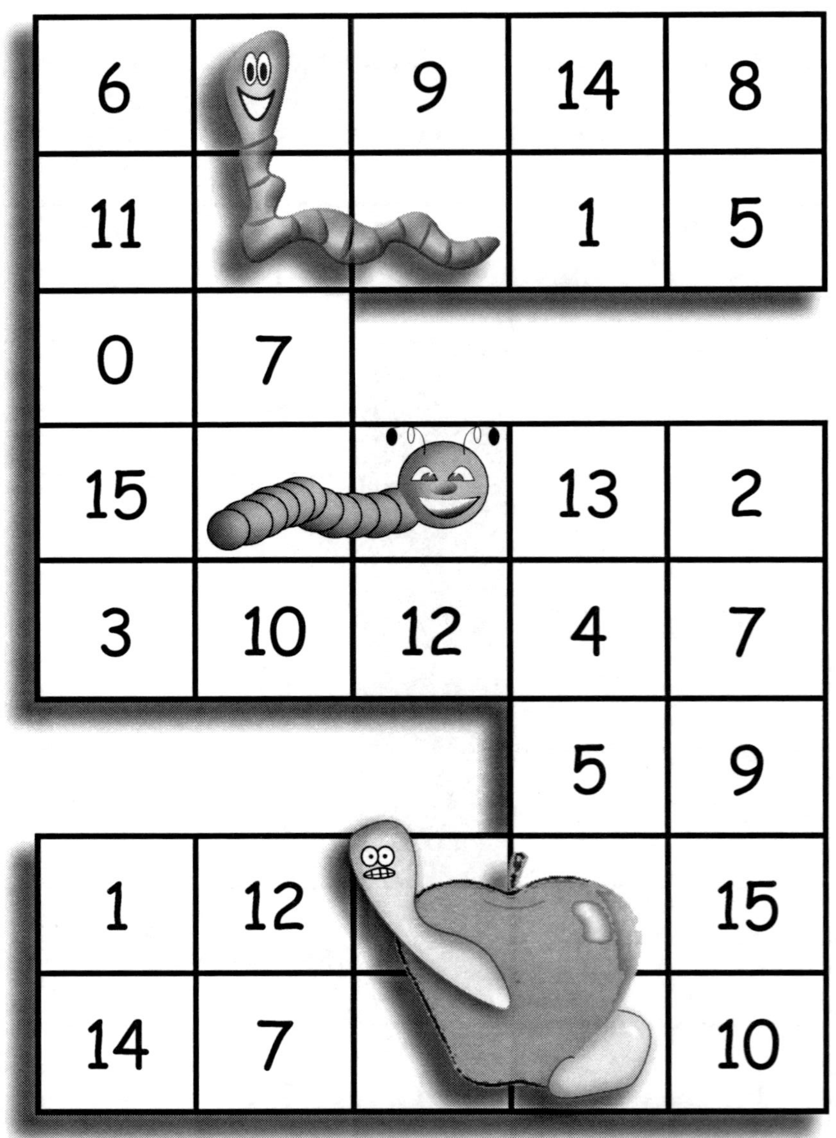

Triple Cross

Focus

Triple Cross is a game for two players which practices recognising, counting and ordering numbers up to ten and adding up to twenty.

What you need

- Playing cards (one each of numbers 1 – 10)
- Counters
- Triple Cross game board

How to play

Firstly, remove one of each card from 1 – 10, shuffle them up and place them in a pile face down between the two players. Player 1 then begins by turning over a card from the pile, in this example a seven.

They must count the number of symbols (spades, hearts, diamonds or clubs) and then say the number on the card. Then they can place a counter of their colour on the matching number on the number track, as shown below.

1	2	3	4	5	6		8	9	10

Player 2 then turns over a card and does the same. Players check each others' counting to make sure it is done correctly. Play continues with both players turning over cards and placing their counters on the number track.

How to win

The first player to get three counters or crosses of their own colour together in a line wins the game. The numbers do not need to be consecutive but must not be separated by a cross of the opponent's colour, as shown in the diagram below.

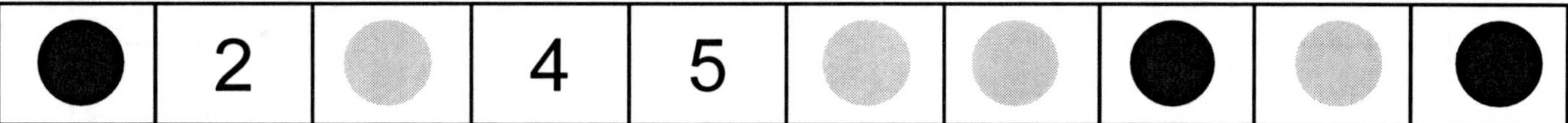

If no player gets three counters together then the game is a draw. Remove the counters, shuffle the cards and play again.

Rule changes / Next steps

- Players have to get three consecutive numbers to win.
- Use the number line with only zero and ten marked at each end. Players have to work out where to put their crosses without the rest of the numbers.
- Use the number track with ten and nineteen marked at each end. Players turn a card and then have to calculate how many more to make twenty (or subtract the value of the card from twenty) before placing a counter on the matching answer.

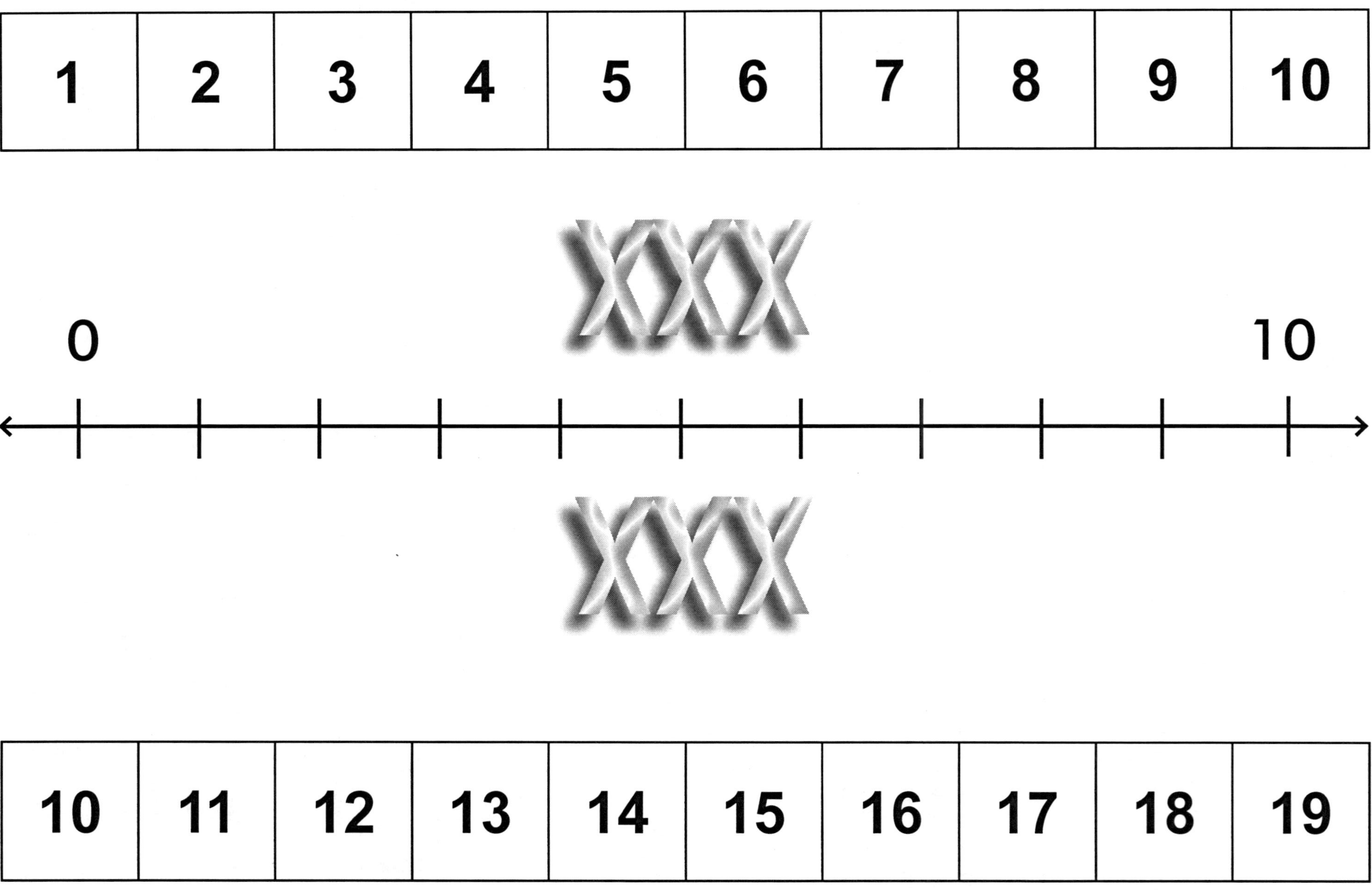
1 2 3 4 5 6 7 8 9 10
0
10
10 11 12 13 14 15 16 17 18 19

Hooked!

Focus

Hooked! is a game for two players which practices adding and subtracting numbers up to twenty.

What you need

- Playing cards (aces, twos and threes only)
- Counter
- Hooked! game board

How to play

The cards are shuffled and placed in a pile, face-down between both players. Decide who is counting forwards and who is counting backwards. The player counting forwards moves from left to right along the game board and the player counting backwards moves from right to left. Place a counter on the middle number of the game board.

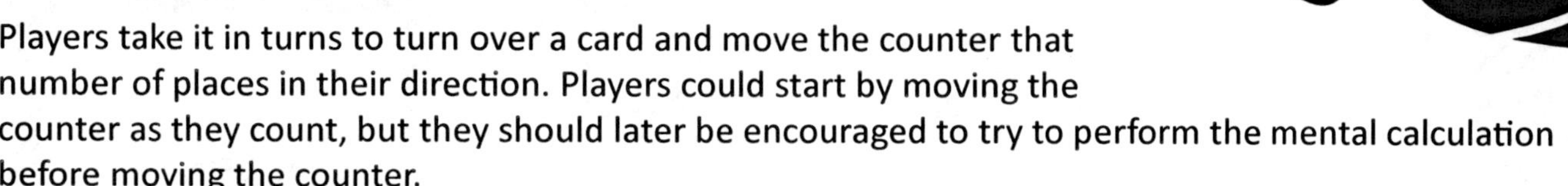

Players take it in turns to turn over a card and move the counter that number of places in their direction. Players could start by moving the counter as they count, but they should later be encouraged to try to perform the mental calculation before moving the counter.

> **For example**
> Player 1 (adding) turns over a three. They say 5 + 3 = 8, and then move to that square on the game board. Player 2 (subtracting) turns over a two. They say 8 – 2 = 6 and moves the counter to square 6.

A correct answer must be given in order to move. When all the cards have been used, shuffle them and place them back down in a pile so that play can continue.

How to win

Player 2 (subtracting) hooks the fish and wins by getting the counter to land on or go past zero whilst Player 1 (adding) hooks the fish and wins by getting the counter to land on or go past ten (or twenty if playing Hooked! 20).

Rule changes / Next steps

- Change roles and play again so both players practice their addition and subtraction skills.
- Play for a set number of turns and the player who is closest to their end of the game board wins.
- Remove the aces (ones) to make the calculations more difficult.
- Use objects such as counters, buttons or even dried beans, to help with calculations. In this way players can progress to more difficult calculations involving adding or subtracting larger numbers, such as 6 – 4 or even 4 + 5, rather than playing with just aces, twos and threes.
- For Hooked! 20 remove only the higher value cards (sevens up to kings) before play.

Hooked
0
10
1
9
2
8
3
4
5
6
7

Hooked
0
1
2
3
4
5
6
7
8
9
10
11
12
13
14
15
16
17
18
19
20

Dare!

Focus

Dare is a game for two or more players which practices adding and subtracting numbers up to twenty.

What you need

- Playing cards (1 – 5)
- Counters (a different colour for each player)
- Dare! game board

How to play

Firstly, the cards are shuffled and placed in a pile, face-down and within reach of all the players. The players' counters are placed on the number twenty on the game board, which is the starting position. Player 1 takes a card and then subtracts this number from the number underneath their counter (which, in this first instance, is twenty), moving their counter to that number on the game board. Player 1 must then decide whether to play safe, stop and pass the cards to the next player or to 'dare' and turn over another card. If Player 1 decides to dare and turn over another card then:

- if the card is the same colour they can continue by subtracting the value of the card from the number underneath their counter;
- if the card is a different colour they must go back to the start.

DARE

If Player 1 decides to stop then play goes to Player 2. Play continues with players taking a card, subtracting its value from the number underneath their counter, and moving their counter to the new total.

Players must do all their mental calculations before moving the counter. If a player gives an incorrect answer then they are unable to move their counter on that turn. If a player lands on top of another counter, the counter landed on is moved back to the start.

How to win

The first player to land on or go past zero (the finish line) is the winner.

Rule changes / Next steps

- For Dare 10 only use cards 1 – 3.
- Play it as an addition game, starting at zero and adding up to the finish line.
- Allow players to count the squares as they move and then record calculations using a whiteboard/ paper and pen.

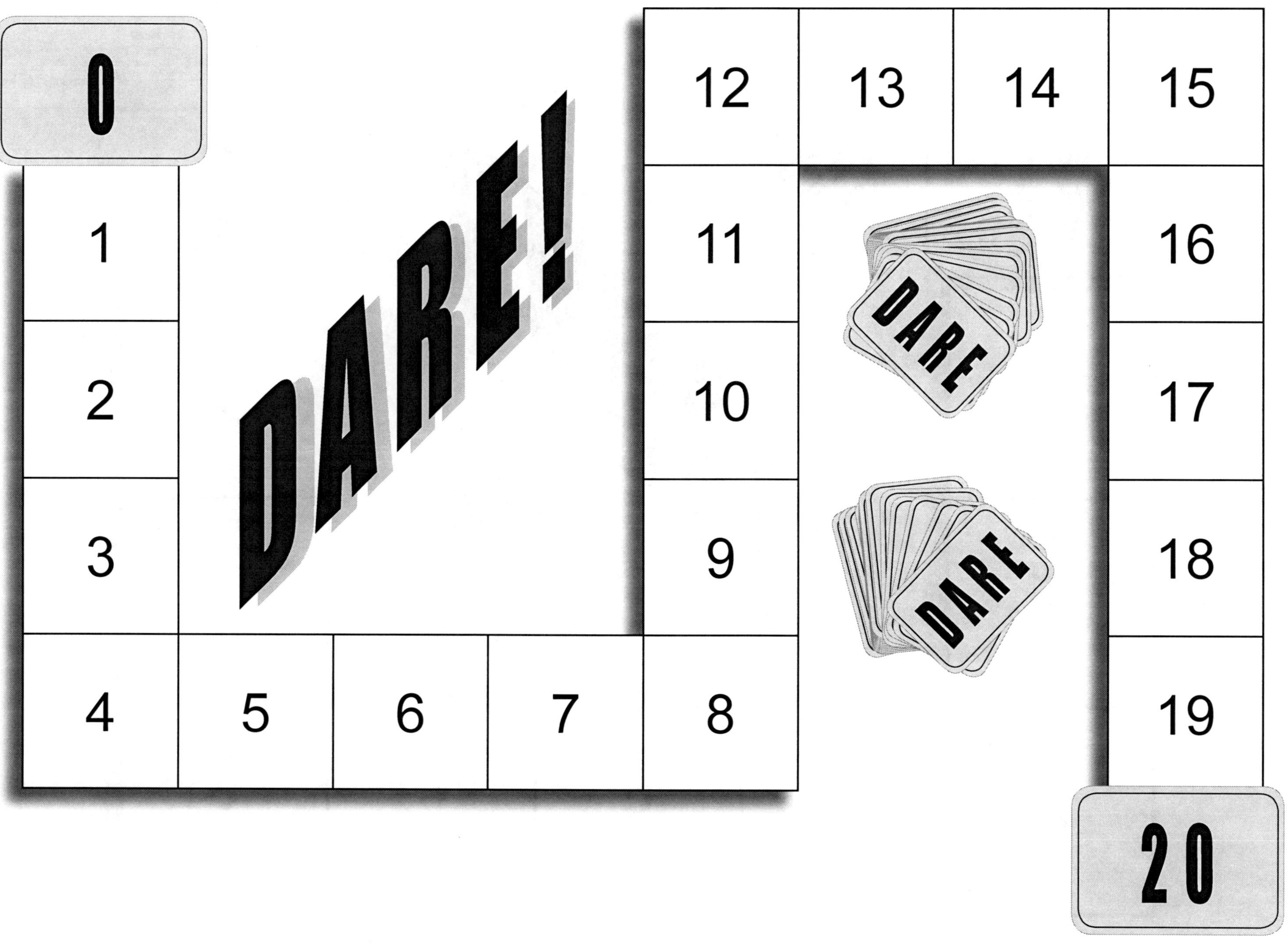
0
DARE!
1
2
3
4
5
6
7
8
9
10
11
12
13
14
15
16
17
18
19
20
DARE
DARE

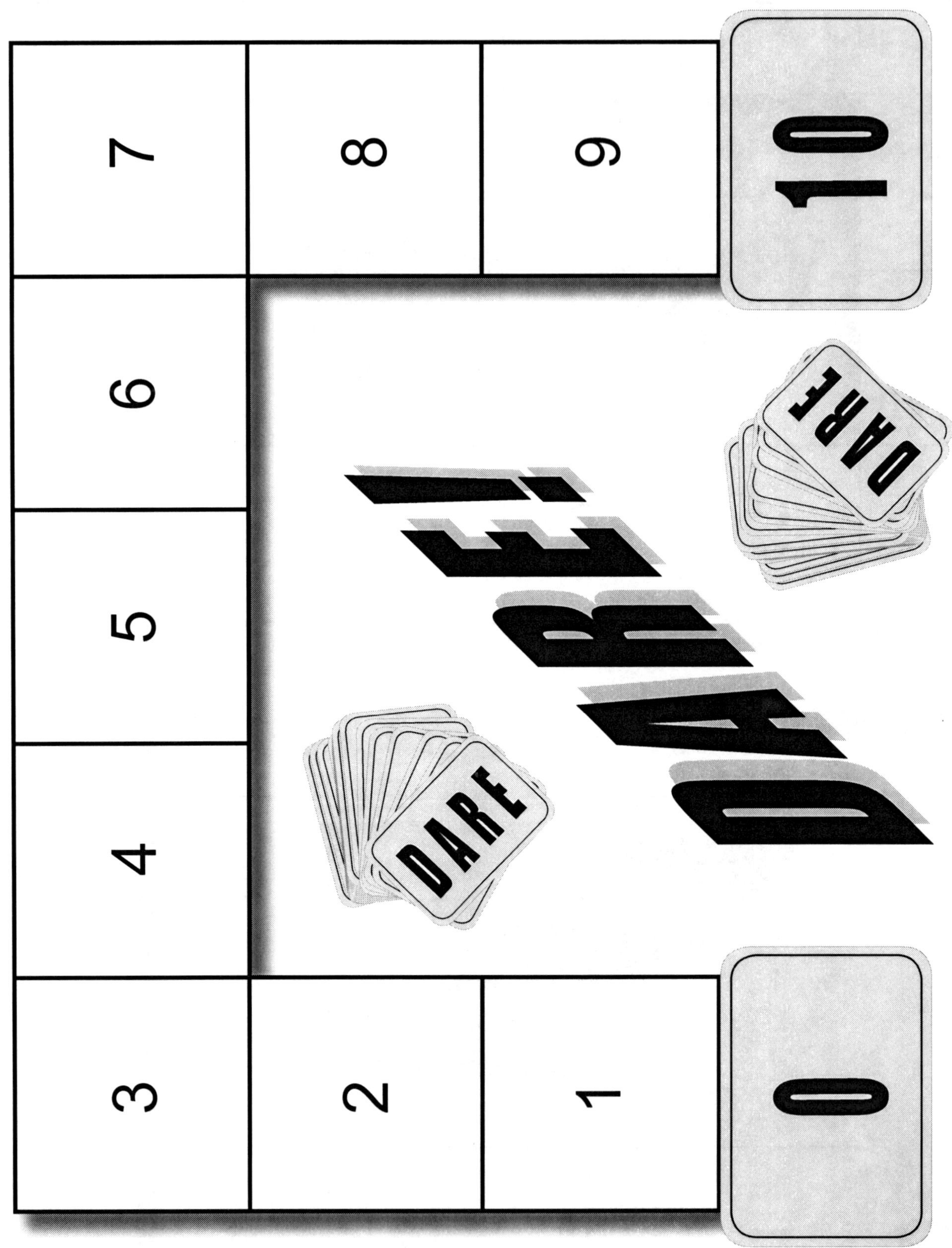
0
1
2
3
4
5
6
7
8
9
10
DARE!
DARE
DARE

Speed Seekers

Focus

Speed Seekers is a game for two or more players which practices adding and subtracting with numbers up to twenty.

What you need

- Playing cards (sixes and above removed)
- Counters (a different colour for each player)
- Speed Seekers game board

How to play

The higher cards are removed from the pack and the remainder are shuffled and placed in a pile, face-down and within reach of all the players. Player 1 takes a card from the top of the pack and subtracts the number on the card from the number under their counter (on the first turn, this is the starting value of twenty). On performing the calculation correctly, they then move their counter to the relevant square on the game board.

For example

Player 1 (grey counter) turns over a four. They calculate 20 – 4 = 16 and move their counter to that position on the game board.

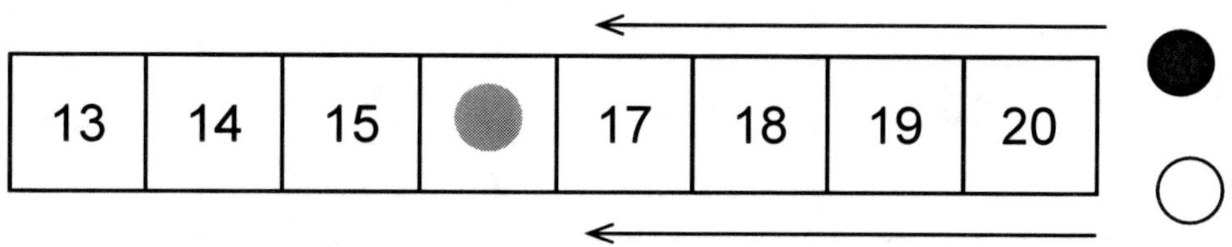

Play goes to Player 2 who turns over a two. Calculating 20 – 2 = 18, they move their counter to number eighteen on the board. Play continues in this way, with players taking a card, and subtracting its value from the number underneath their counter.

Players must do all their mental calculations before moving their counter. They must also give the correct answer to move their counter otherwise it remains where it is on the game board.

If a player lands on top of another counter, the counter landed on is moved back to the start.

How to win

The first player to land on or go past zero (the finish line) on the game board is the winner.

Rule changes / Next steps

- For Speed Seekers 10 the cards from four and above are removed from the pack.
- Play as an addition game, starting at the lower number and adding up to the finish line.

SPEED SEEKERS

0 1 2 3 4 5 6 7 8 9 10 11 12 13 14 15 16 17 18 19 20

SPEED SEEKERS
10
0
1
2
9
3
8
4
5
6
7

Snapjack

Focus

Snapjack is a game for two players which practices adding and subtracting one-digit numbers whilst recognising odd and even numbers up to twenty.

What you need

- Playing cards (kings and queens removed)

How to play

When the kings and queens have been removed from the pack, all the remaining cards are dealt out equally between the two players and are placed in a pile face down in front of them. Both players must then turn over their top two cards, quickly and at the same time. The players must add both their own cards together to get a total and those of their partner to get another total. If the card totals are both even or both odd then the first player to say 'Snap' wins all the cards in front of both players. The winner of that round puts these cards on the bottom of their pile and then the players continue to turn over two of their cards at the same time.

Play continues with both players trying to be the first to say 'Snap' when matching odd or even totals appear. When a player gets to the last card in their pile they just pick them up, turn them face down and start again with the top card. However, if a player gets left with only one or two cards, with no more to turn over, then the card(s) is left face up on the table. The other player keeps turning cards until a matching odd or even total appears and a call of 'Snap' is made.

If either player turns over a Jack the first player to call 'Snapjack' instantly wins the cards in the piles of both players. If the first player to call out only says 'Snap' then this doesn't count and the game continues.

How to win

A player wins the game if they get all the cards in the pack or they have the most cards after a set amount of time.

Rule changes / Next steps

- If a player says 'Snap' or 'Snapjack' at the wrong time then their opponent wins the cards.
- Players have to find the difference between their two cards and if both differences are odd or even then 'Snap' can be called.
- Leave the picture cards in the pack so that more difficult calculations have to be performed or remove cards above six for simpler ones. The rule for calling 'Snapjack' still applies.

Kings

Focus

Kings is a game for two or more players which practices adding and subtracting numbers up to 20. It can also be used to read and compare two-digit numbers up to 100.

What you need

- Playing cards (queens and jacks removed)

How to play

When the queens and jacks have been removed from the pack, lay out all the remaining cards face-down, in rows and in reach of all the players. Each player picks up any two cards and adds them together. Players take it in turns to put their cards down in front of them and say their total. The player with the highest total takes all the cards from each player and puts them face down in one pile in front of them. If two or more players have the same total then each player must work out the difference between the numbers on their cards. In this case the player who has the largest difference wins all the cards.

For example

Player 1

Player 2

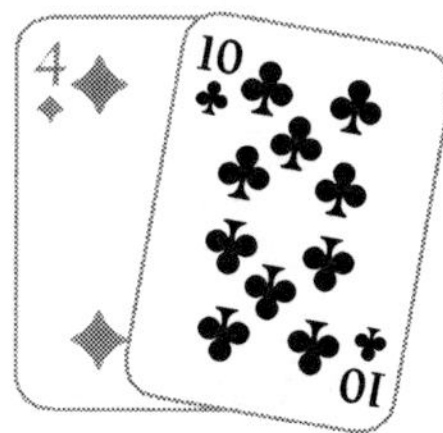

Player 3

Both Player 1 and Player 3 below have picked up cards that give them the same total score of fourteen. However, Player 3 has a difference of six between the cards and Player 1 has a difference of two between their cards. Therefore, Player 3 wins all the cards for this round.

Players continue to take two cards and find the totals, the player with the highest total winning the cards. If a player picks up a king they automatically win that round and if two or more players pick up a king then the player with the highest other card wins. Keep playing until there are not enough cards on the table for another round.

How to win

The player with the most cards in front of them at the end of the game is the winner.

Rule changes / Next steps

- Players find the difference between their two cards and the player with the biggest difference wins the round. If two or more players have the same difference then the higher total wins.
- Add the other picture cards for more difficult calculations.
- Players pick two cards and make the largest two-digit number they can. Players say their numbers as they put them down and the player with the largest number wins the cards. A king represents one hundred so wins the round if selected. If two players choose a king then the player with the other highest card still wins that round.

Trios

Focus

Trios is a game for four to six players which can be used to practice becoming more efficient in a range of mental methods with numbers up to twenty.

What you need

- Playing cards
- Counters (a different colour for each player)
- Trios game board

How to play

Player 1 turns over any number of cards and could be asked to add or subtract them to get an answer, depending on what skill or knowledge from the Year 1 programme of study the game is being used to practice. If the player gets the answer correct they can place a counter of their own colour in a circle on the game board.

Player 2 then turns over one or more cards and performs a similar calculation. Play continues in this way with players taking it in turns to take one or more cards, answer questions and place counters on the game board. If a player gives an incorrect answer, they are unable to place a counter on that turn.

How to win

The first player to make a Trio is the winner. Trios can either be in a triangle or in a straight line as shown in the diagram.

Remove all the counters and play again.

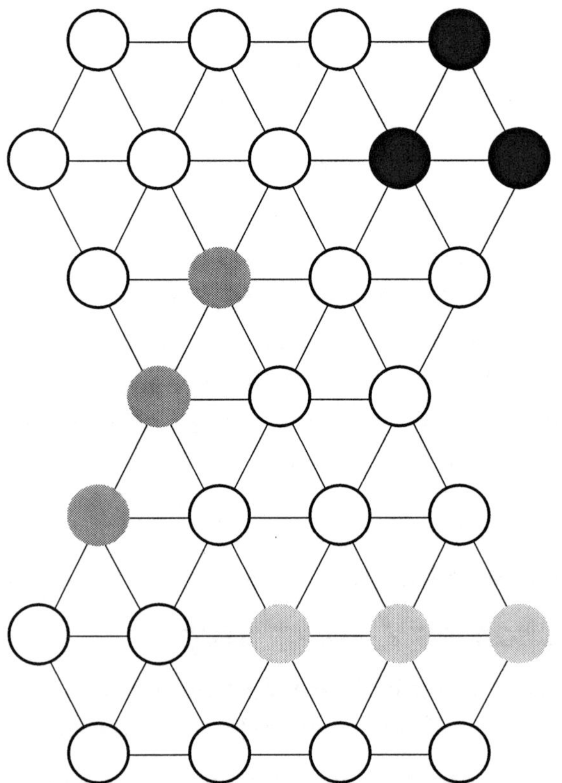

Rule changes / Next steps

- Players continue to try and make Trios until all the spaces are covered or until the players agree that no more can be made. Players score three points for every Trio they make and the winner is the player with the most points at the end of the game.
- Restrict players to making only triangles or straight lines to win the game rather than allowing both.

TRIOS

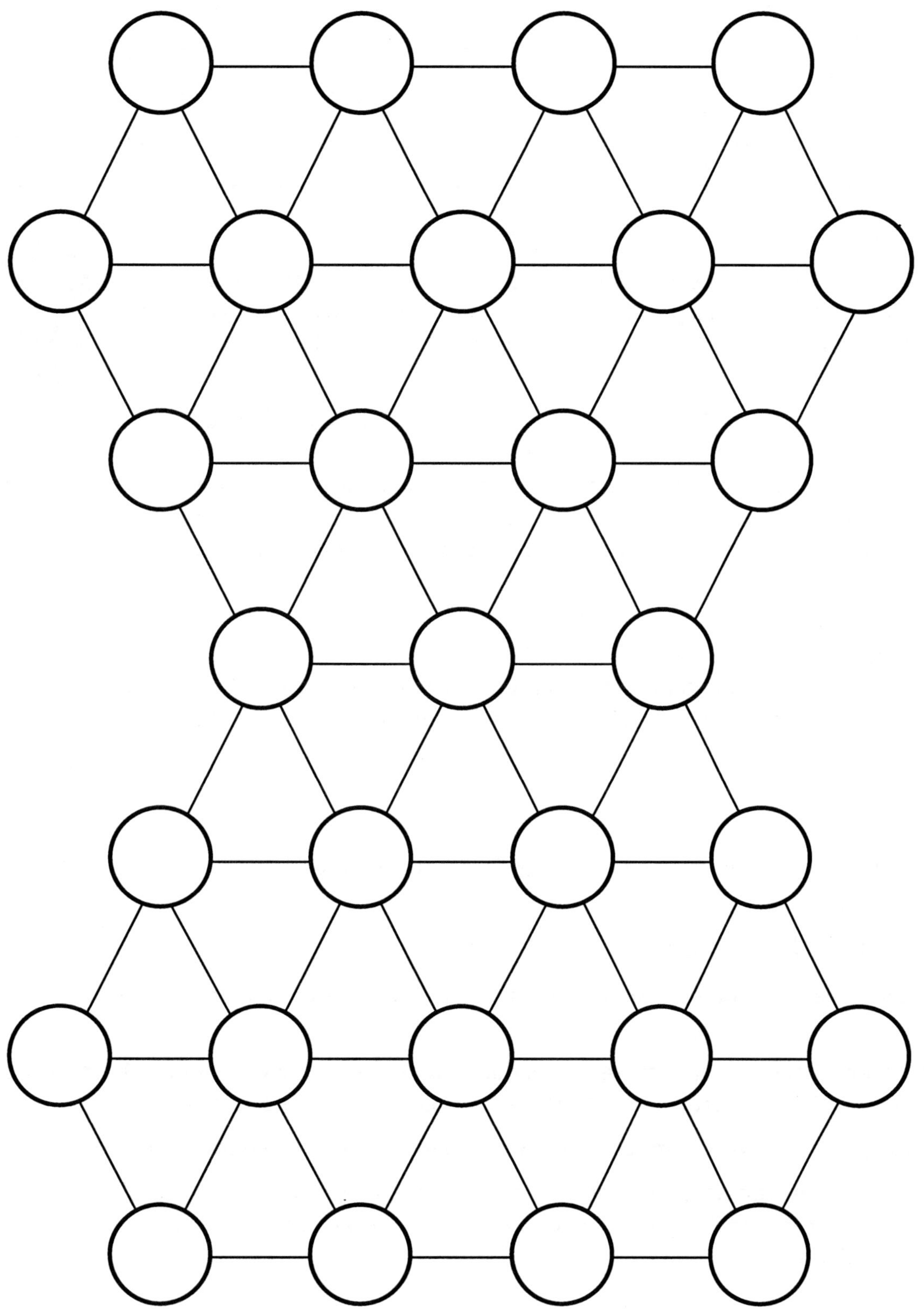

Monster Mash-Up

Focus

Monster Mash-up is a game for two to six players which can be used to practice becoming more efficient in a range of mental methods with numbers up to one hundred.

What you need

- Playing cards (cards 1–5)
- Counters (one for each player)
- Monster Mash-Up game board
- Question cards, if using (see Next Steps, below)

How to play

When the cards from six upwards have been removed from the pack the remaining cards are shuffled and placed in a pile, face-down and within reach of all the players. Players then choose a monster and place their counter on it, ready for the start of the game.

Player 1 is asked a question by the question master to practice recall of facts or any skill within the Year 1 programme of study. If answered correctly Player 1 turns over a card and can then move the same number of spaces on the game board. If the answer is incorrect the player is not allowed to move their counter. The other players are then asked questions in turn. If correct they can turn over a card and move the same number of spaces on the game board.

Black holes

Players must try and avoid the black holes in various positions on the game board, since landing on one sends them back to their monster at the start of the game.

How to win

The first player to land on or go beyond an end square is the winner.

Rule changes / Next steps

- Players can move one bonus square if they can answer a question that another player has answered incorrectly.
- Different kinds of question may be selected, dependent, for example, on what a particular child needs to practice, or on particular skills needed for assessment purposes.
- Players must turn the exact number to land on an end square and win the game.
- Use the set of mixed mental questions provided. Put them face-down on the table for children to pick at random, read aloud and then answer. Alternatively, pass them to an appointed question master to read out.

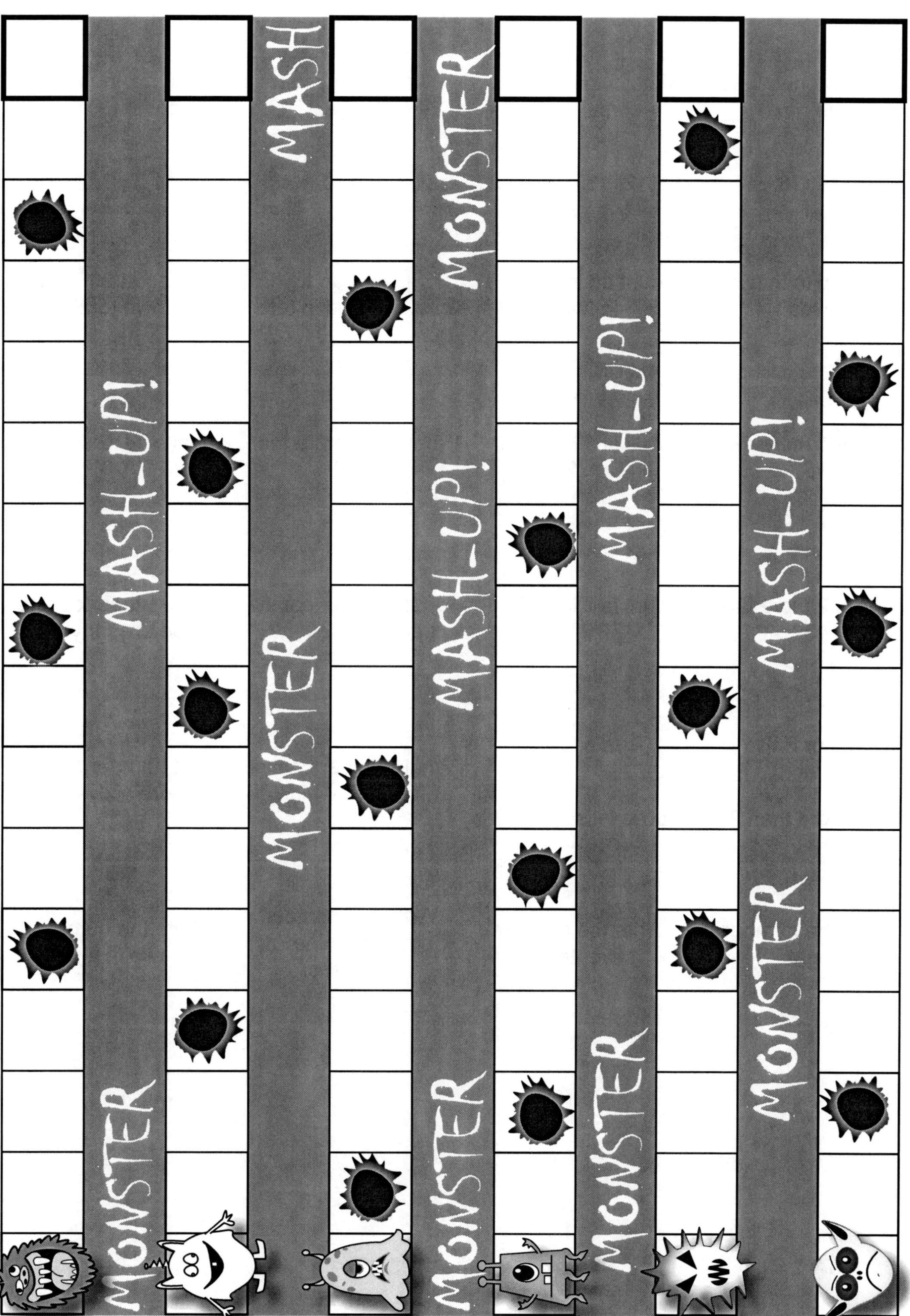
MONSTER MASH-UP!
MONSTER MASH-UP!
MONSTER MASH-UP!
MONSTER MASH-UP!
MONSTER MASH-UP!

What two numbers come next? 15, 16, 17, 18, …, …	What two numbers come next? 13, 12, 11, 10, …, …	What two numbers come next? 2, 4, 6, 8, …, …	What two numbers come next? 13, 11, 9, 7, …, …
Count up to thirty in fives	Count up to sixteen in twos	Count up to one hundred in tens	Starting at 30, count down to 20
What is 1 more than 18?	What is 1 less than 11?	What is 10 more than 20?	What is 10 less than 70?
What is 2 more than 13?	What is 2 less than 6?	What number comes after fifty-seven?	What number comes before forty?
True or False 36 is more than 25	True or False 50 is less than 62	What number comes after eighty-nine?	What number comes before sixty-six?
Write the number eight.	Write the number seventeen.	Write the number twenty-nine in figures.	Write the number forty-two in figures.
2 + 3 =	7 + 1 =	8 = 6 + __	10 = 5 + __
6 – 2 =	4 – 0 =	5 = 6 – __	2 = 4 – __

12 + 4 =	3 + 10 =	16 + 0 =	7 + 11 =
15 – 5 =	11 – 9 =	20 – 2 =	14 – 4 =
Add 7 and 4	Add 1 and 15	What is the total of 3 and 5?	What is the total of 2 and 12?
Take 3 away from 10	Take 4 away from 16	What is the difference between seven and nine?	What is the differ-ence between ten and twenty?
What is 6 more than 1?	What is 5 more than 10?	What is 3 less than 8?	What is 4 less than 19?
Double 3	Double 10	I doubled a number and got a total of four. What number did I double?	Double __ = 8
If I had two groups of five objects, how many would I have altogether?	If I had two groups of two objects, how many would I have altogether?	How many equal groups of two can I make from these ten counters?	How many equal groups of three can I make from these nine counters?
Find ½ of these eight counters	Find ½ of these twelve counters	Find ¼ of these eight counters	Find ¼ of these twelve counters

Tarquin Mathematics Resources

Tarquin has more than a thousand product lines to support and enrich mathematics. You can browse them at **www.tarquingroup.com**.

To make it easy to buy what you need to really use this book, we have some special packages online — put the keyword ACE into the quick search box to see the full range at once.

- Packs of Playing Cards - Special ACE prices
- Coloured Counters
- Beads

Other Tarquin Products designed for you

Books

First Tables Colouring Book

Second Tables Colouring Book

Arithmetic Arithmetic

Mathematical Vocabulary 1

and many, many more ...

Posters

One Million Poster

Multiples Poster

Equal Parts Poster

and many, many more ...

Dice and other Manipulatives

Excellent prices on 12-sided and 10-sided dice classroom packs — ideal for mental mathematics

Practical Arithmetic and Operations Dice Packs

Pentominoes, tangrams, Cuisenaire Rods, Polygons and much much more.

Tarquin, Suite 74, 17 Holywell Hill, St Albans, AL1 1DT
Tel: +44 (0)1727833866 Fax: +44 (0)845 456 6385
www.tarquingroup.com Follow us on Twitter @TarquinGroup

Lightning Source UK Ltd.
Milton Keynes UK
UKOW02f0156180615

253690UK00003B/5/P

9 781907 550911